The Jesus Prayer

with 77 Christian Crosses Colouring Book

For Christian Meditation and Spiritual Healing

ESTHER PINCINI

The Jesus Prayer with 77 Christian Crosses Colouring Book
For Christian Meditation and Spiritual Healing
by Esther Pincini

Copyright © Magdalene Press 2018

ISBN 978-1-77335-111-7

No part of this publication may be reproduced, stored in a retrieval system, or transmitted in any form or by any means, electronic, mechanical, photocopying, recording or otherwise without written permission of the publisher.

Magdalene Press, September 2018

Lord Jesus Christ, my Saviour, Son of God, have mercy on me.

Lord Jesus Christ, my Saviour, Son of God, have mercy on me.

Lord Jesus Christ, my Saviour, Son of God, have mercy on me.

Lord Jesus Christ, my Saviour, Son of God, have mercy on me.

Lord Jesus Christ, my Saviour, Son of God, have mercy on me.

Lord Jesus Christ, my Saviour, Son of God, have mercy on me.

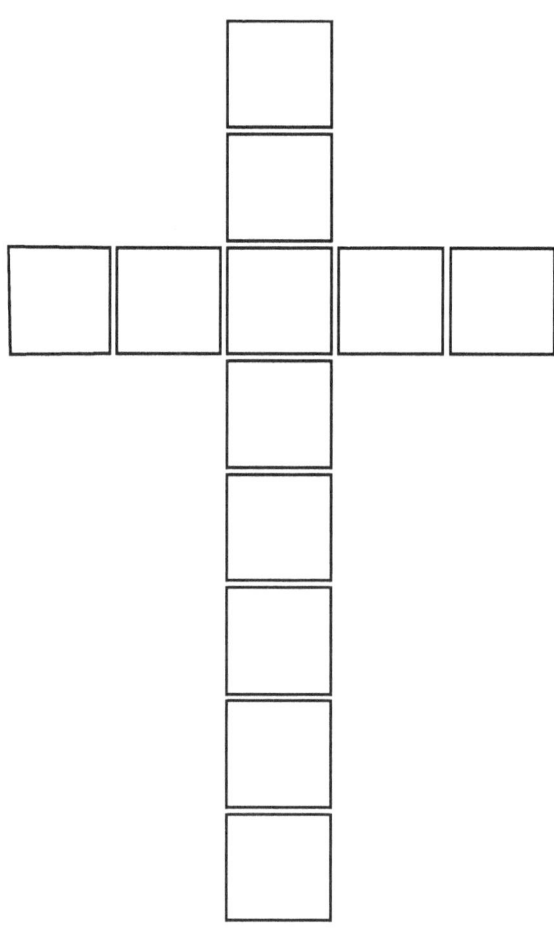

Lord Jesus Christ, my Saviour, Son of God, have mercy on me.

Lord Jesus Christ, my Saviour, Son of God, have mercy on me.

Lord Jesus Christ, my Saviour, Son of God, have mercy on me.

Lord Jesus Christ, my Saviour, Son of God, have mercy on me.

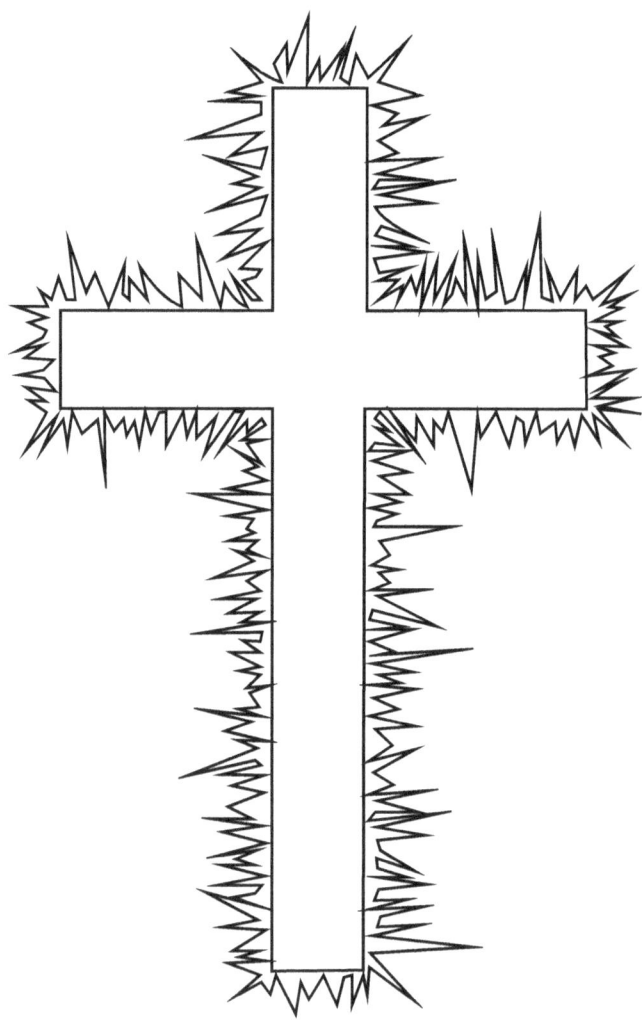

Lord Jesus Christ, my Saviour, Son of God, have mercy on me.

Lord Jesus Christ, my Saviour, Son of God, have mercy on me.

Lord Jesus Christ, my Saviour, Son of God, have mercy on me.

Lord Jesus Christ, my Saviour, Son of God, have mercy on me.

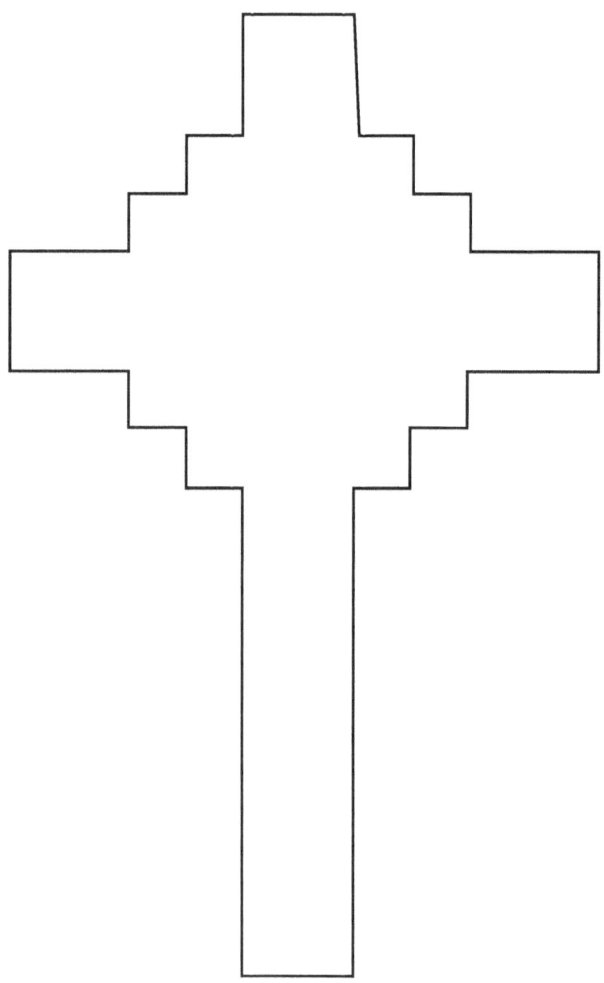

Lord Jesus Christ, my Saviour, Son of God, have mercy on me.

Lord Jesus Christ, my Saviour, Son of God, have mercy on me.

Lord Jesus Christ, my Saviour, Son of God, have mercy on me.

Lord Jesus Christ, my Saviour, Son of God, have mercy on me.

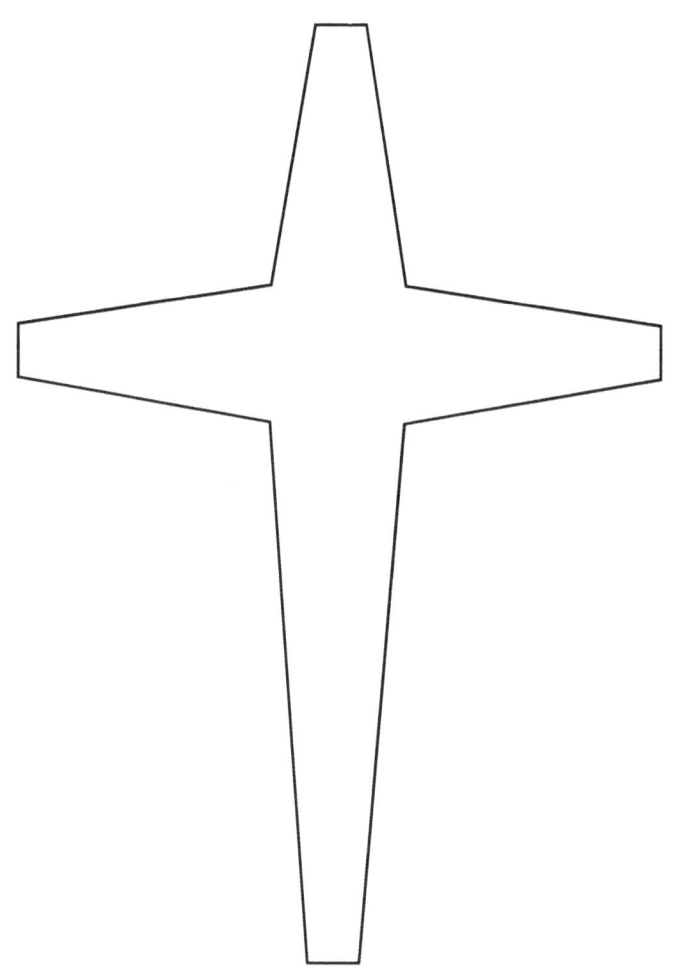

Lord Jesus Christ, my Saviour, Son of God, have mercy on me.

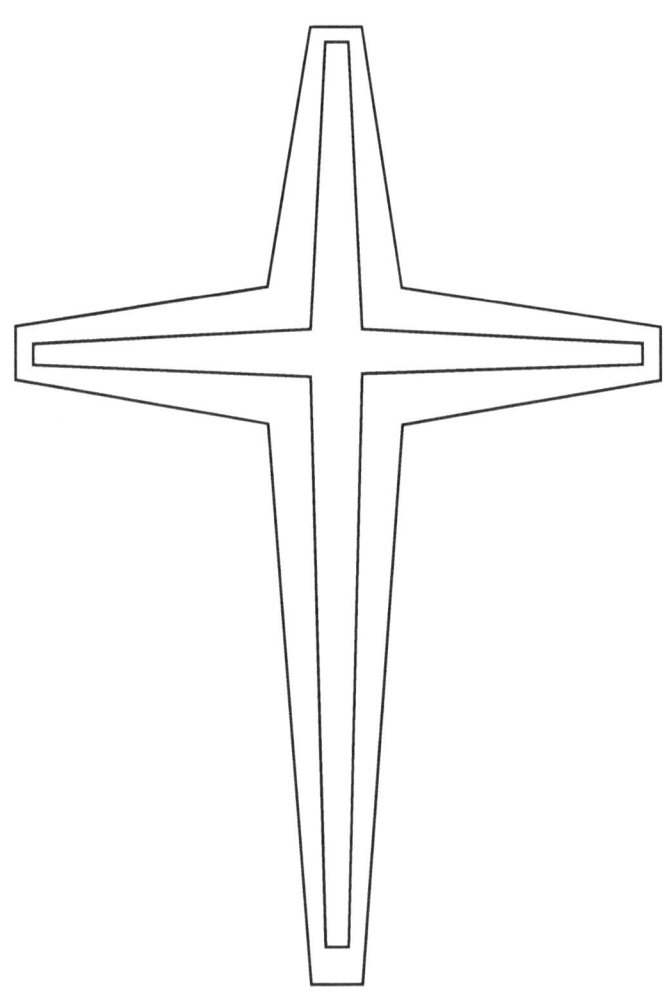

Lord Jesus Christ, my Saviour, Son of God, have mercy on me.

Lord Jesus Christ, my Saviour, Son of God, have mercy on me.

Lord Jesus Christ, my Saviour, Son of God, have mercy on me.

Lord Jesus Christ, my Saviour, Son of God, have mercy on me.

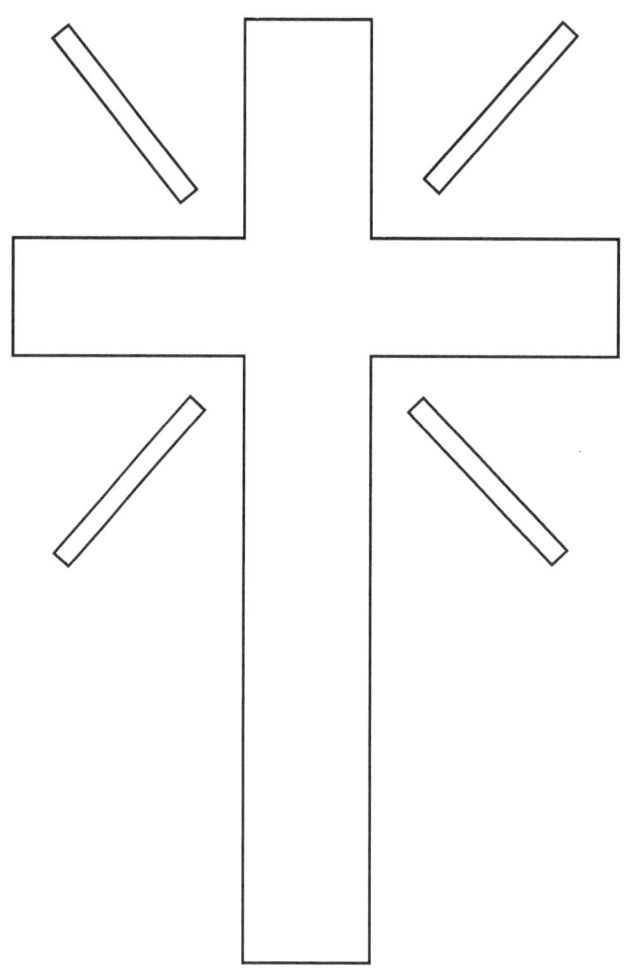

Lord Jesus Christ, my Saviour, Son of God, have mercy on me.

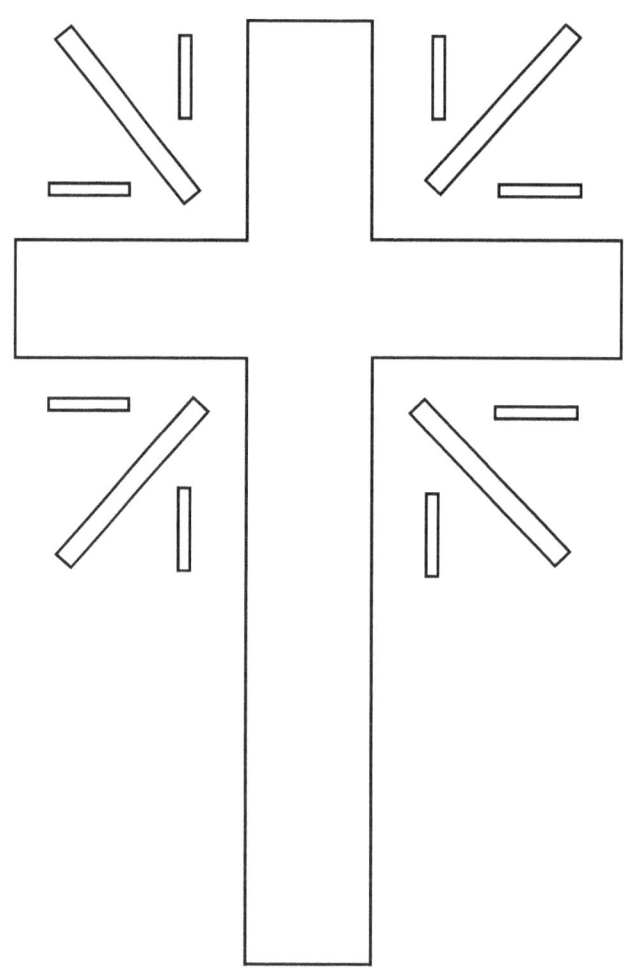

Lord Jesus Christ, my Saviour, Son of God, have mercy on me.

Lord Jesus Christ, my Saviour, Son of God, have mercy on me.

Lord Jesus Christ, my Saviour, Son of God, have mercy on me.

Lord Jesus Christ, my Saviour, Son of God, have mercy on me.

Lord Jesus Christ, my Saviour, Son of God, have mercy on me.

Lord Jesus Christ, my Saviour, Son of God, have mercy on me.

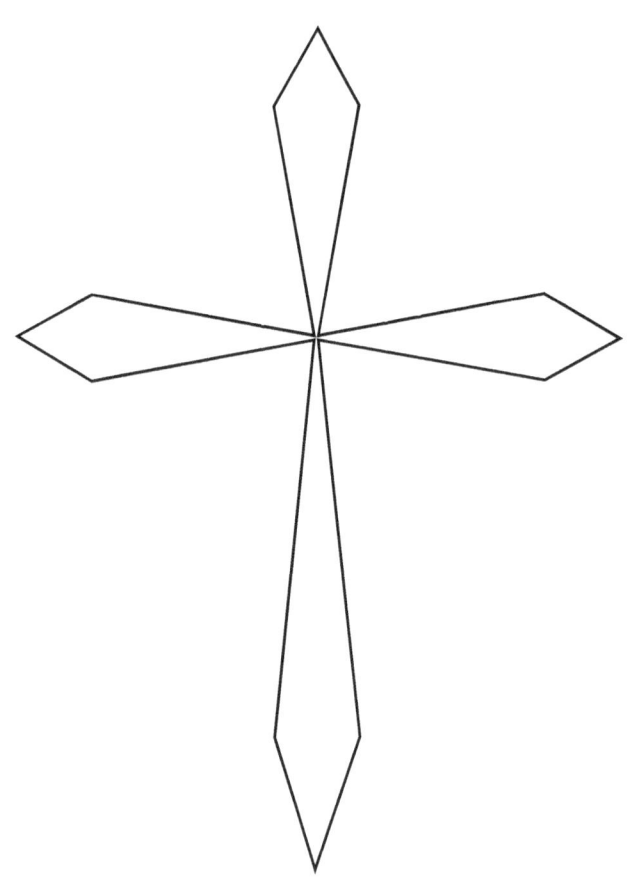

Lord Jesus Christ, my Saviour, Son of God, have mercy on me.

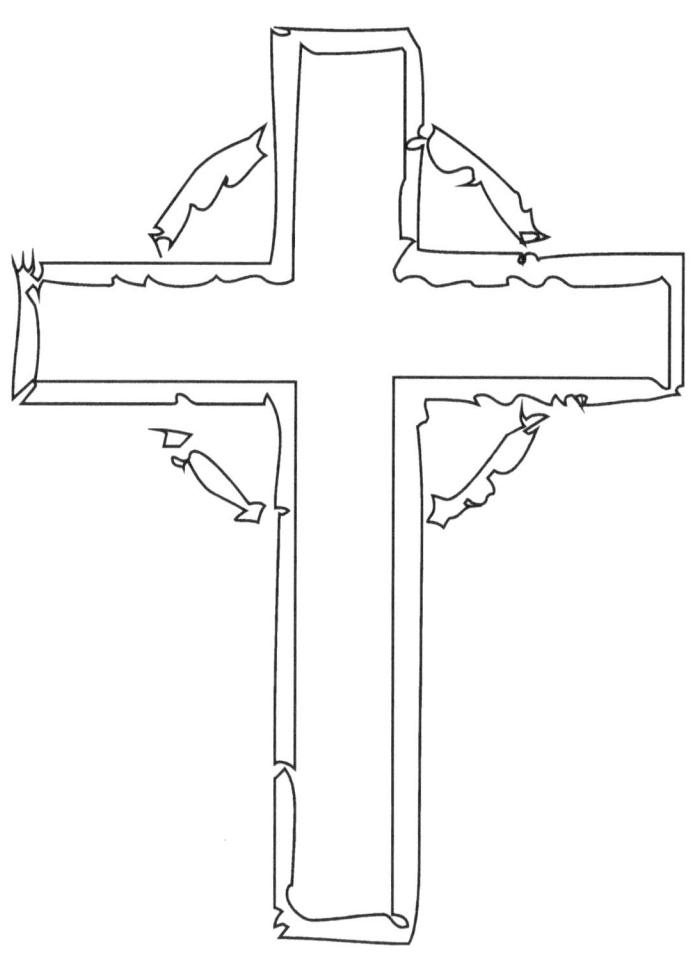

Lord Jesus Christ, my Saviour, Son of God, have mercy on me.

Lord Jesus Christ, my Saviour, Son of God, have mercy on me.

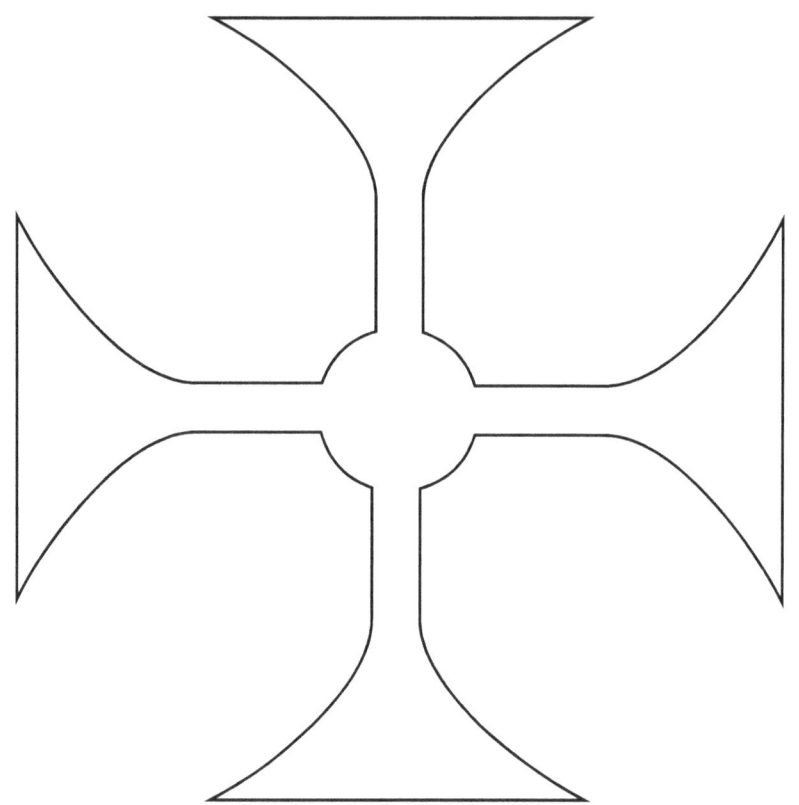

Lord Jesus Christ, my Saviour, Son of God, have mercy on me.

Lord Jesus Christ, my Saviour, Son of God, have mercy on me.

Lord Jesus Christ, my Saviour, Son of God, have mercy on me.

Lord Jesus Christ, my Saviour, Son of God, have mercy on me.

Lord Jesus Christ, my Saviour, Son of God, have mercy on me.

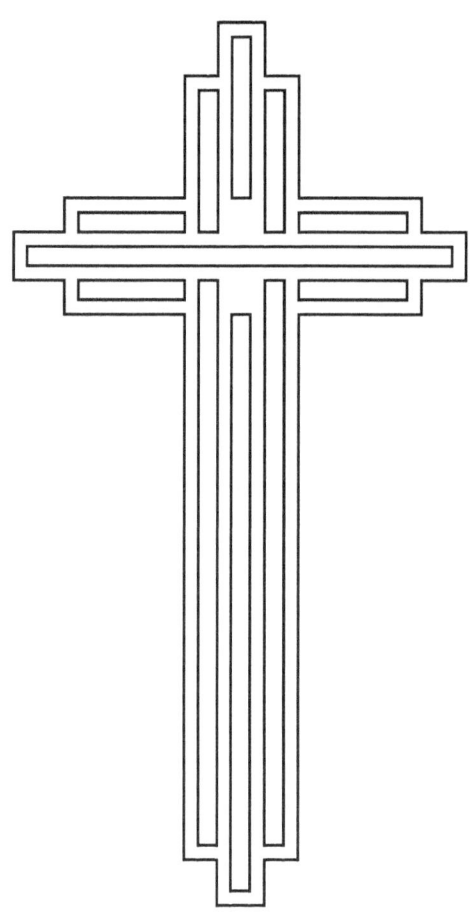

Lord Jesus Christ, my Saviour, Son of God, have mercy on me.

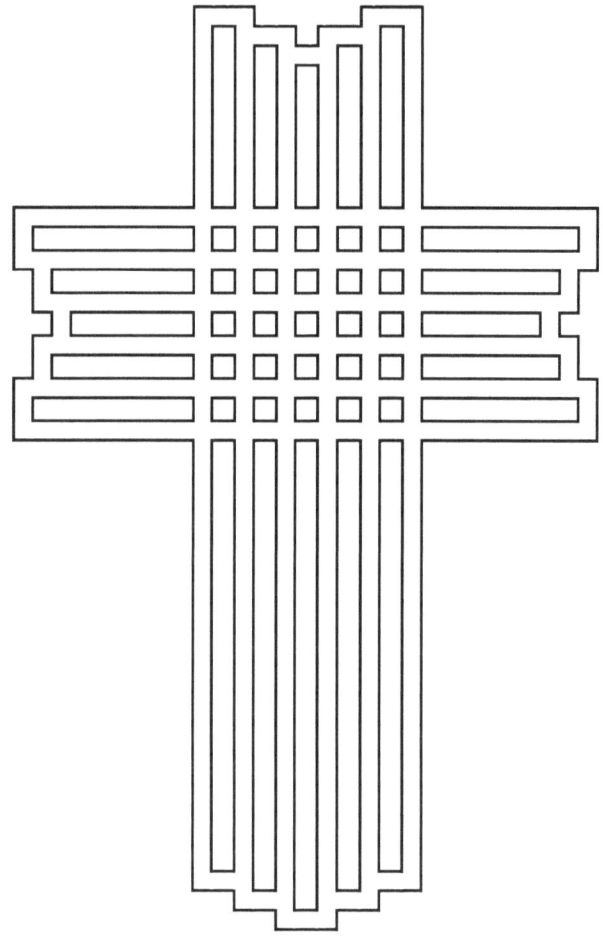

Lord Jesus Christ, my Saviour, Son of God, have mercy on me.

Lord Jesus Christ, my Saviour, Son of God, have mercy on me.

Lord Jesus Christ, my Saviour, Son of God, have mercy on me.

Lord Jesus Christ, my Saviour, Son of God, have mercy on me.

Lord Jesus Christ, my Saviour, Son of God, have mercy on me.

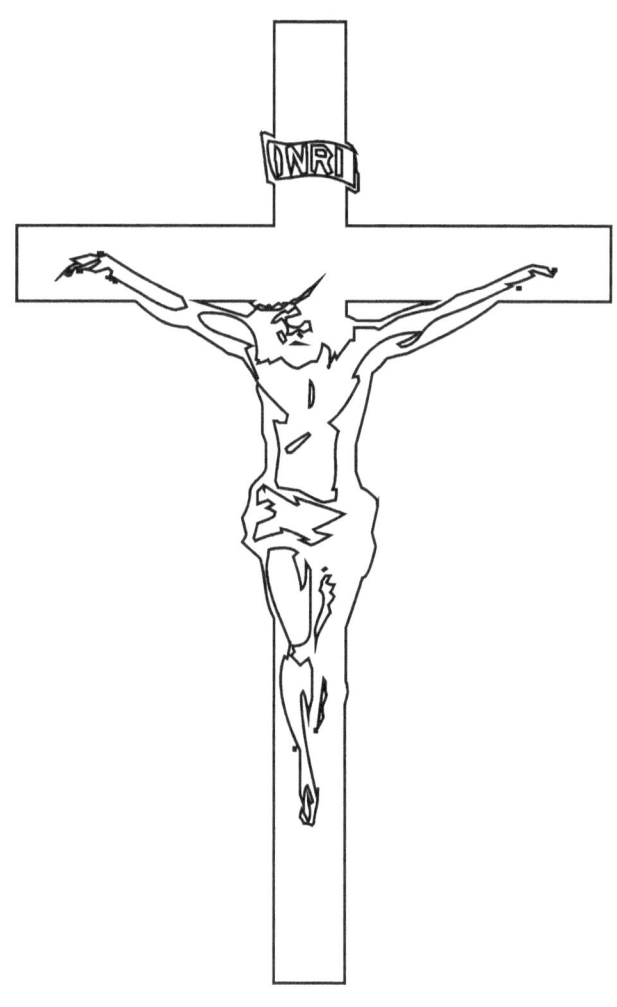

Lord Jesus Christ, my Saviour, Son of God, have mercy on me.

Lord Jesus Christ, my Saviour, Son of God, have mercy on me.

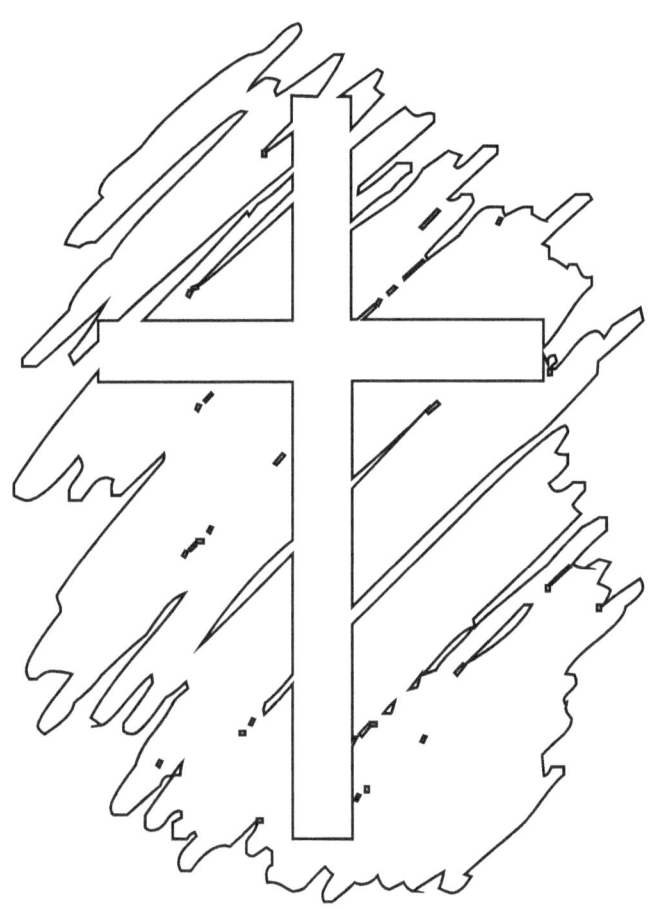

Lord Jesus Christ, my Saviour, Son of God, have mercy on me.

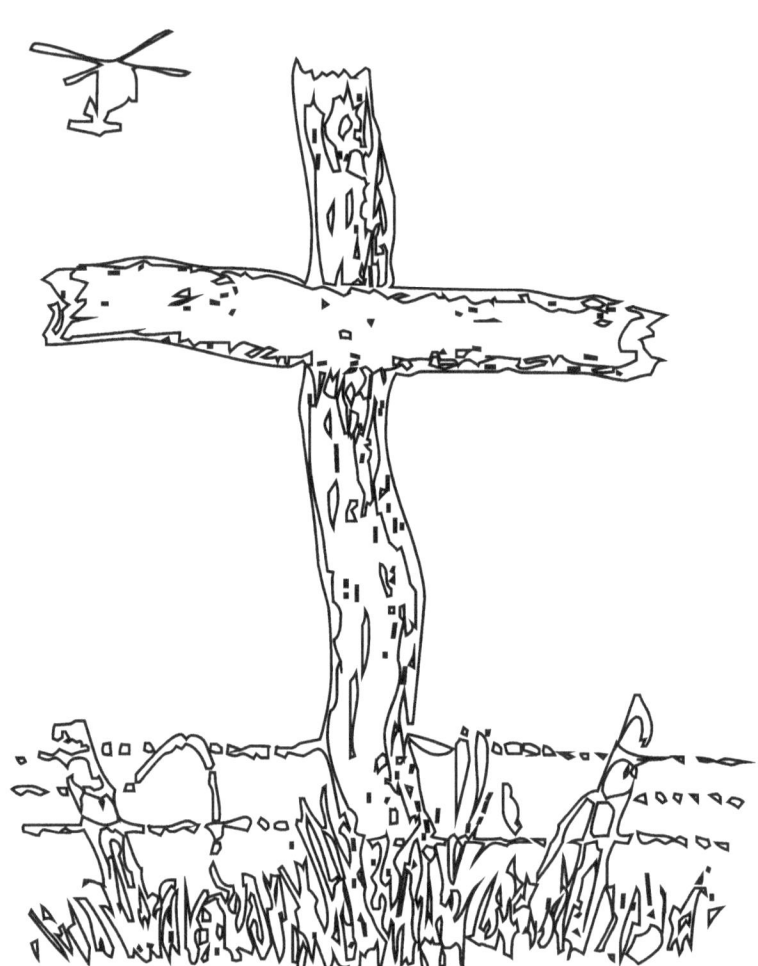

Lord Jesus Christ, my Saviour, Son of God, have mercy on me.

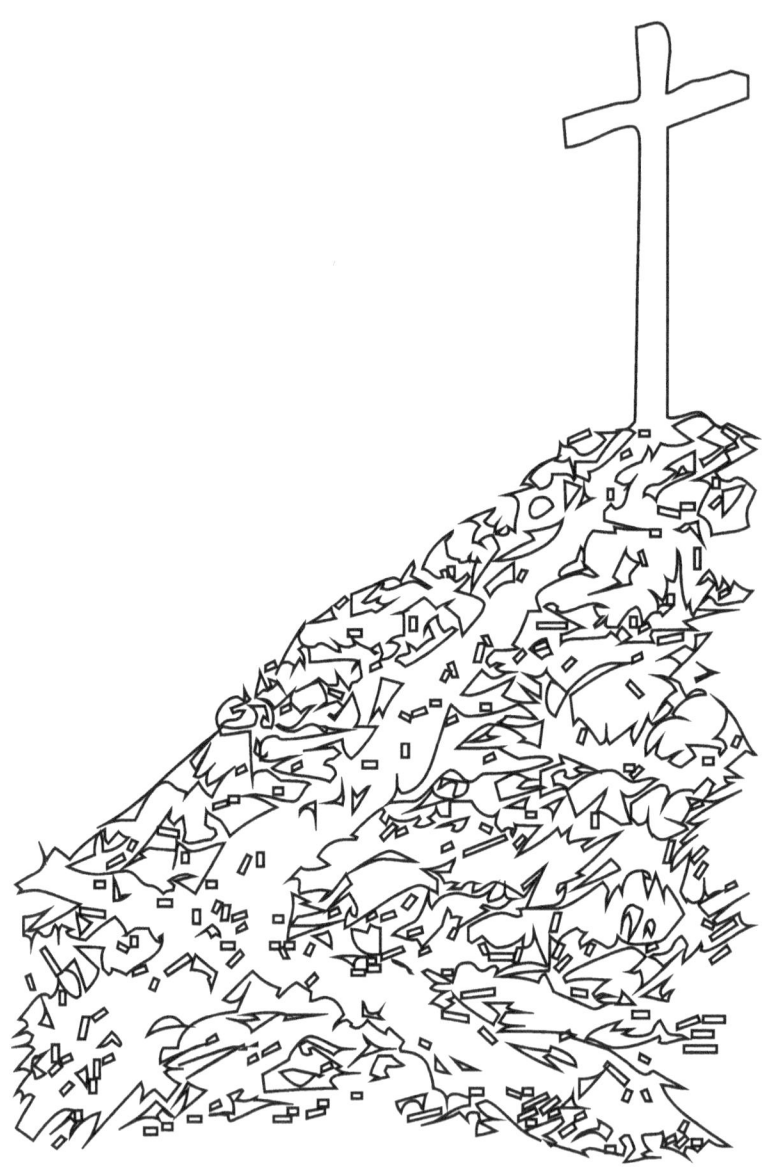

Lord Jesus Christ, my Saviour, Son of God, have mercy on me.

Lord Jesus Christ, my Saviour, Son of God, have mercy on me.

Lord Jesus Christ, my Saviour, Son of God, have mercy on me.

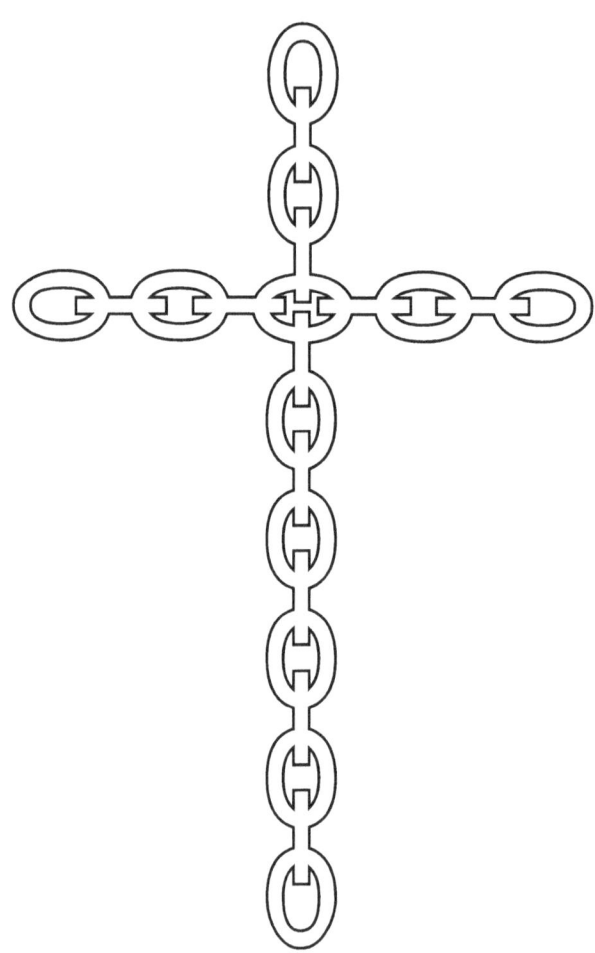

Lord Jesus Christ, my Saviour, Son of God, have mercy on me.

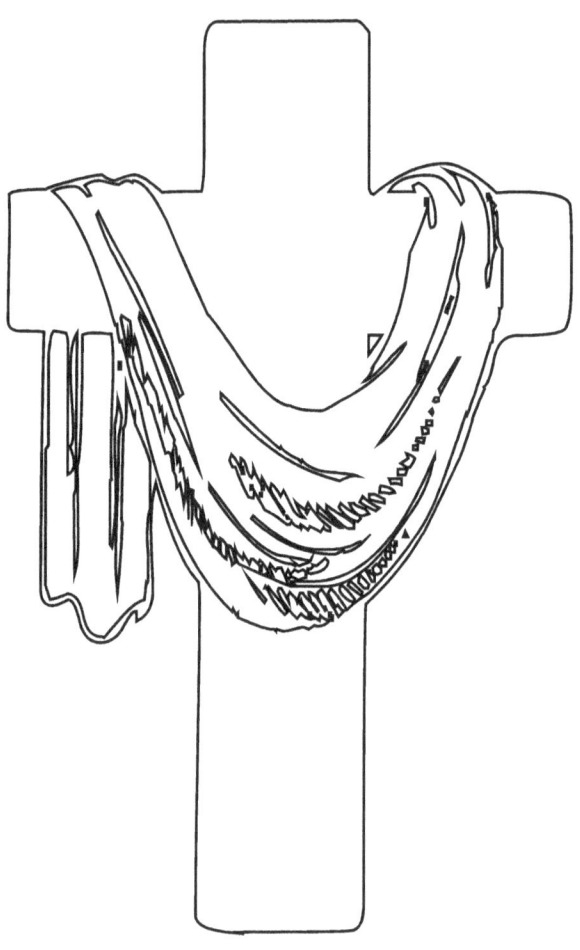

Lord Jesus Christ, my Saviour, Son of God, have mercy on me.

Lord Jesus Christ, my Saviour, Son of God, have mercy on me.

Lord Jesus Christ, my Saviour, Son of God, have mercy on me.

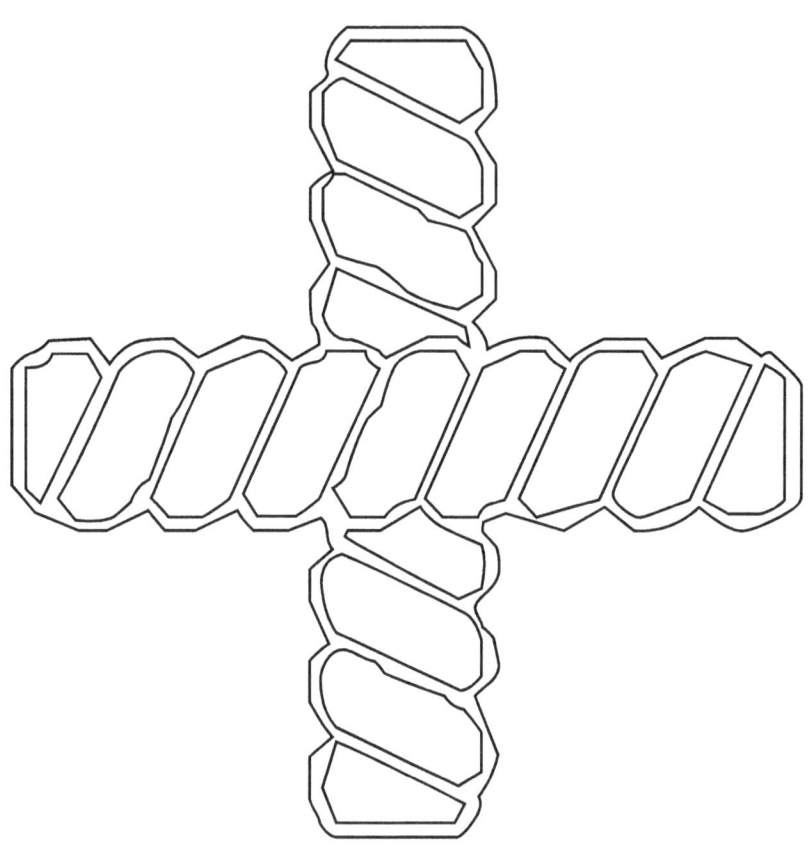

Lord Jesus Christ, my Saviour, Son of God, have mercy on me.

Lord Jesus Christ, my Saviour, Son of God, have mercy on me.

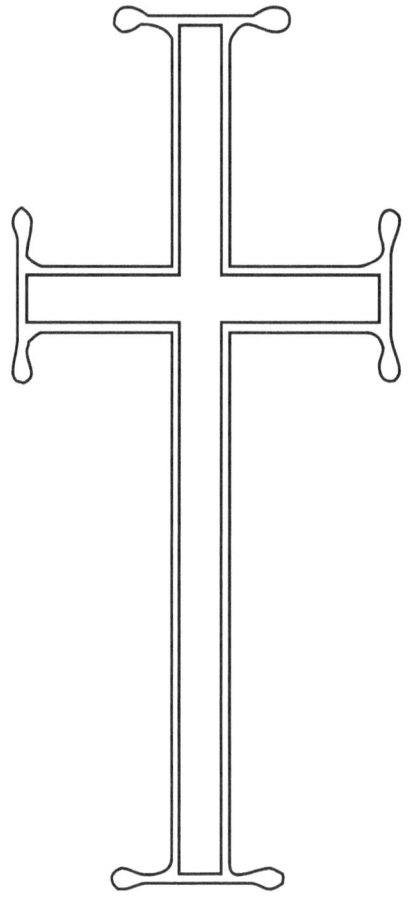

Lord Jesus Christ, my Saviour, Son of God, have mercy on me.

Lord Jesus Christ, my Saviour, Son of God, have mercy on me.

Lord Jesus Christ, my Saviour, Son of God, have mercy on me.

Lord Jesus Christ, my Saviour, Son of God, have mercy on me.

Lord Jesus Christ, my Saviour, Son of God, have mercy on me.

Lord Jesus Christ, my Saviour, Son of God, have mercy on me.

Lord Jesus Christ, my Saviour, Son of God, have mercy on me.

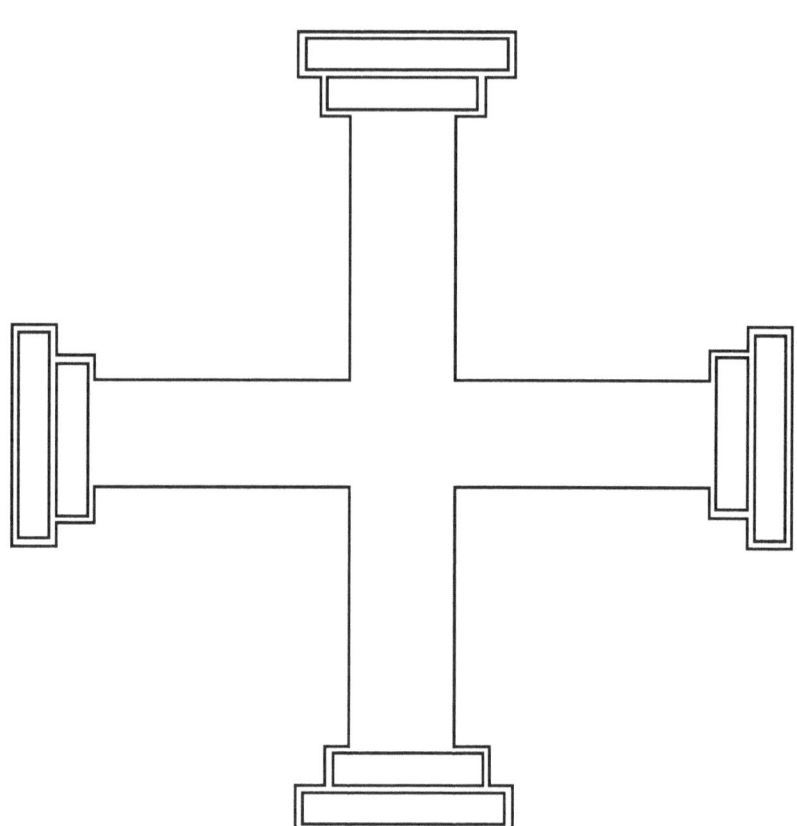

Lord Jesus Christ, my Saviour, Son of God, have mercy on me.

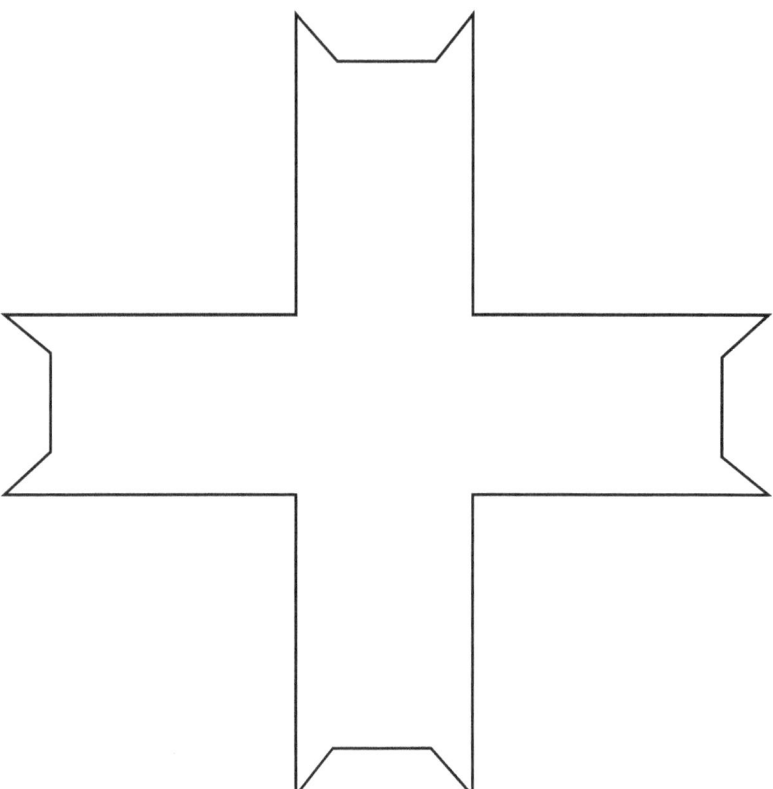

Lord Jesus Christ, my Saviour, Son of God, have mercy on me.

Lord Jesus Christ, my Saviour, Son of God, have mercy on me.

Lord Jesus Christ, my Saviour, Son of God, have mercy on me.

Lord Jesus Christ, my Saviour, Son of God, have mercy on me.

Lord Jesus Christ, my Saviour, Son of God, have mercy on me.

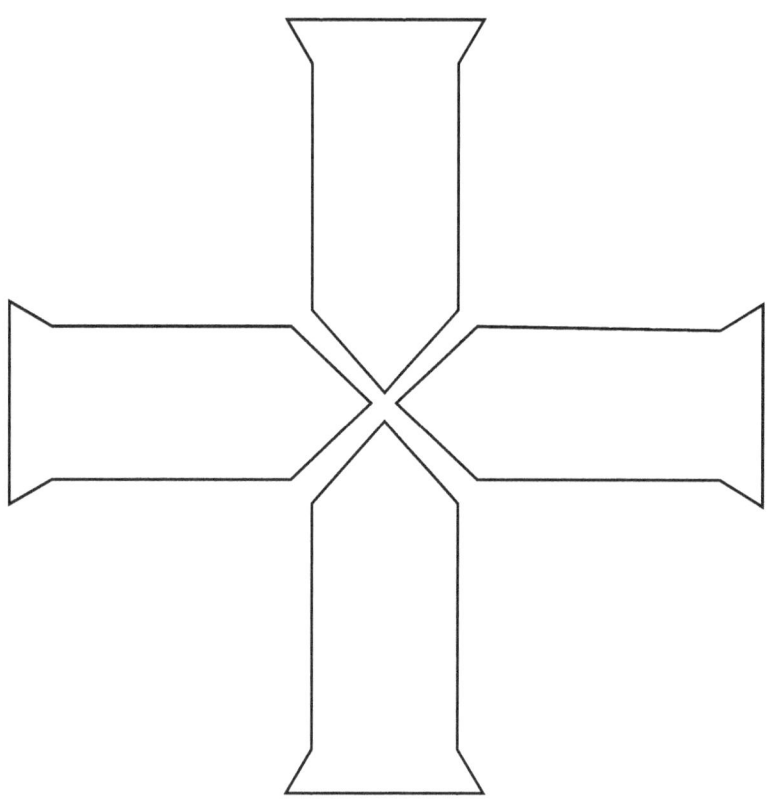

Lord Jesus Christ, my Saviour, Son of God, have mercy on me.

Lord Jesus Christ, my Saviour, Son of God, have mercy on me.

Lord Jesus Christ, my Saviour, Son of God, have mercy on me.

Lord Jesus Christ, my Saviour, Son of God, have mercy on me.

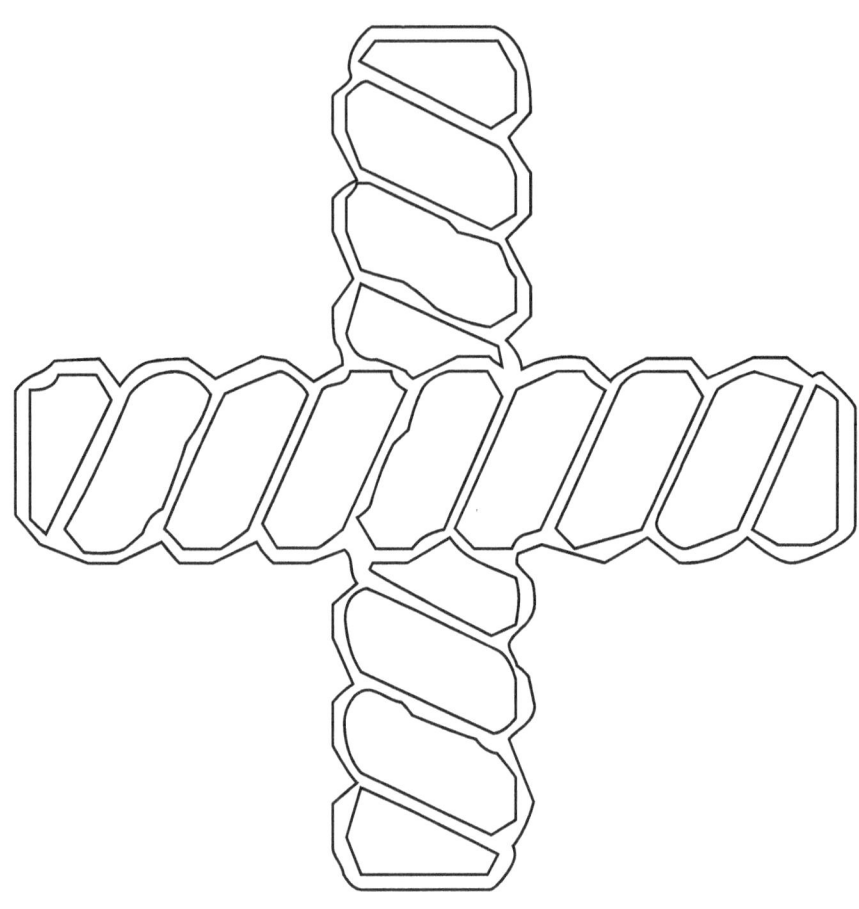

Lord Jesus Christ, my Saviour, Son of God, have mercy on me.

Lord Jesus Christ, my Saviour, Son of God, have mercy on me.

Lord Jesus Christ, my Saviour, Son of God, have mercy on me.

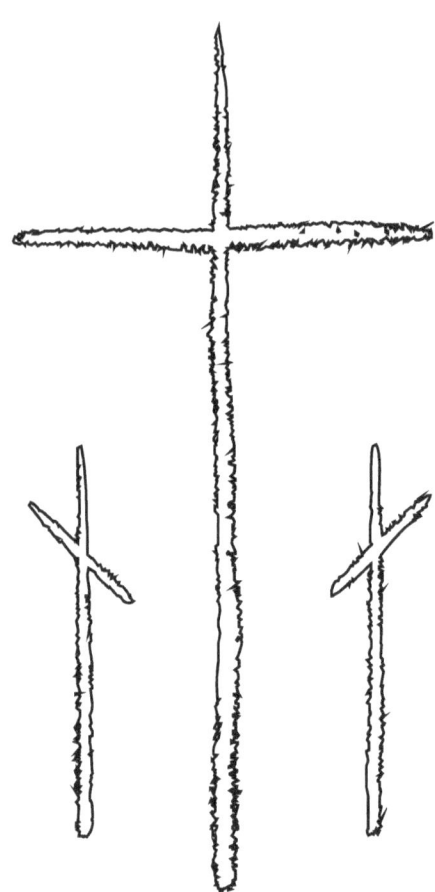

www.ingramcontent.com/pod-product-compliance
Lightning Source LLC
Chambersburg PA
CBHW051119110526
44589CB00026B/2981